John Trumbull

Painter of the
Revolutionary War

John Trumbull

Painter of the Revolutionary War

Stuart A.P. Murray

Sharpe Focus
an imprint of M.E. Sharpe, Inc.

SERIES CONSULTANT

Jeffrey W. Allison
Paul Mellon Collection
Educator, Virginia Museum of Fine Arts

Cover Art:
The Death of General Mercer at the Battle of Princeton (John Trumbull);
engraving of *The Death of General Warren at the Battle of Bunker's Hill,
June 17, 1775* (John Trumbull).

Sharpe Focus
An imprint of M.E. Sharpe, Inc.
80 Business Park Drive
Armonk, NY 10504
www.sharpe-focus.com

Copyright © 2009 by M.E. Sharpe, Inc.

Series created by Kid Graphica, LLC
Series designed by Gilda Hannah

Map: Mapping Specialists Limited

Library of Congress Cataloging-in-Publication Data

Murray, Stuart, 1948–
John Trumbull: painter of the Revolutionary War / Stuart A. P. Murray.
        p. cm—(Show me America)
Includes bibliographical references and index.
ISBN 978-0-7656-8150-8 (hardcover: alk. paper)
1. Trumbull, John, 1756–1843—Juvenile literature. 2. United
States—History—Revolution, 1775–1783—Art and the revolution—
Juvenile literature. 3. United States—History—Revolution, 1775–1783—
Biography—Juvenile literature. 4. Painters—United States—Biography
—Juvenile literature. 5. United States. Army—Biography—Juvenile
literature. I. Title.

ND237.T8M87 2009
759.13—dc22   2008003235

Printed in Malaysia

9 8 7 6 5 4 3 2 1

Contents

By and About John Trumbull   7

Map   8

CHAPTER ONE
A Natural Genius for Art   10

CHAPTER TWO
The Patriot Colonel   18

CHAPTER THREE
An American Artist   26

CHAPTER FOUR
Studio and Prison   34

CHAPTER FIVE
Portraying the Revolution's Finest Moments   40

CHAPTER SIX
A World of Revolution and War   54

CHAPTER SEVEN
An Artist and a Gentleman   62

Glossary   73

Time Line   74

Further Research   75

Bibliography   76

Index   77

By and About John Trumbull

The greatest motive I had or have for engaging in or for continuing my pursuit of painting has been the wish of commemorating the great events of our country's Revolution.

—John Trumbull

By the time John Trumbull, the "patriot-artist," came to live at New Haven in 1837 he had become a legend. One can well imagine a fond father pointing out to his son the tall, erect Colonel, who still retained his fine military bearing, and proudly saying: "There, my boy, goes Colonel Trumbull, General Washington's aide-de-camp!" This scene might have taken place on the elm-shaded streets of New Haven in 1840, nearly one and a half generations after the "glorious year" of 1775. Trumbull was a living embodiment of a heroic past. This, to the aged veteran, was soul satisfying.

—Theodore Sizer, editor,
The Autobiography of Colonel John Trumbull,
(1953 edition preface)

On numerous paintings connected with our Revolutionary history, Colonel Trumbull's fame as an artist may securely rest.

—Samuel F.B. Morse, Eulogy, November 1843

To his country he gave his sword and pencil.

—Trumbull's inscription on his memorial

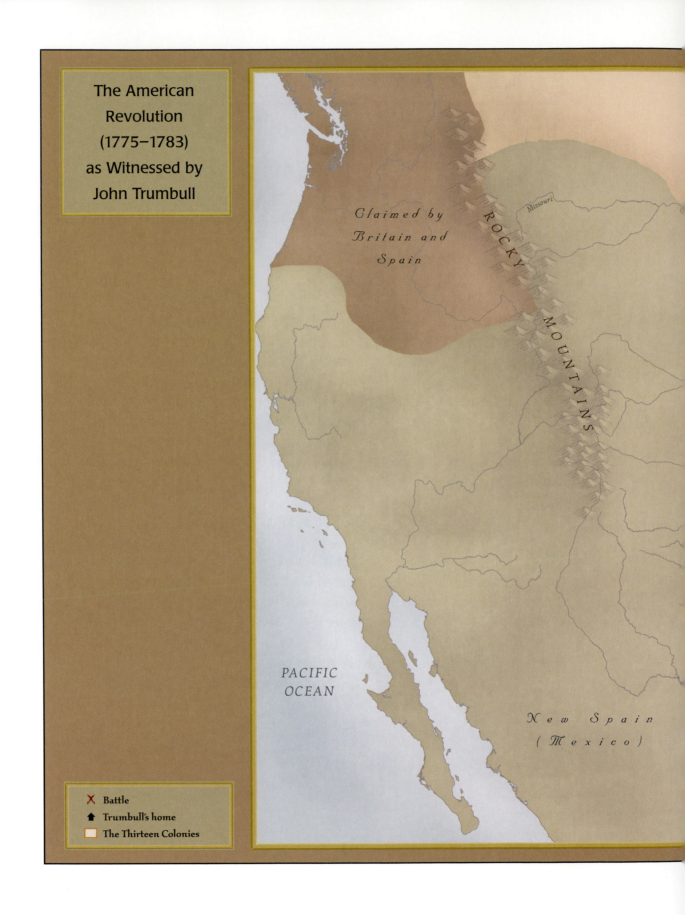

The American
Revolution
(1775–1783)
as Witnessed by
John Trumbull

Claimed by
Britain and
Spain

R O C K Y

M O U N T A I N S

Missouri

PACIFIC
OCEAN

New Spain
(Mexico)

X Battle
⬧ Trumbull's home
☐ The Thirteen Colonies

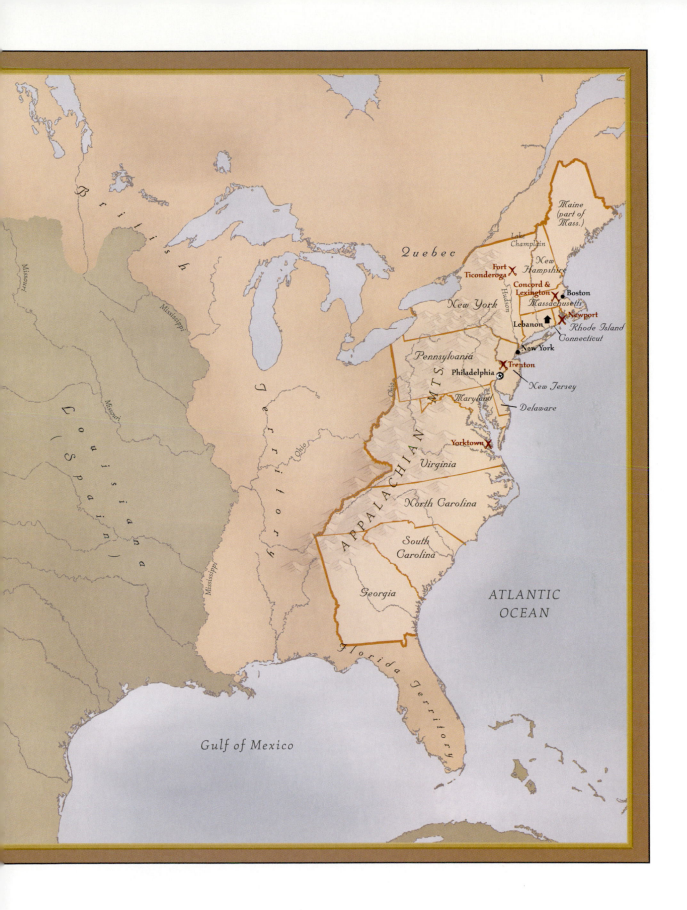

British

Missouri

Mississippi

Quebec

Louisiana
(Spain)

Missouri

Territory

Ohio

Mississippi

APPALACHIAN MTS.

Lake
Champlain

Maine
(part of
Mass.)

New
Hampshire

Fort
Ticonderoga X

New York

Hudson

Concord &
Lexington X • **Boston**
Massachusetts

Lebanon ■

X **Newport**
Rhode Island
Connecticut

• New York

Pennsylvania

X **Trenton**

Philadelphia ⊛

New Jersey

Maryland

Delaware

Yorktown X

Virginia

North Carolina

South
Carolina

Georgia

Florida Territory

ATLANTIC
OCEAN

Gulf of Mexico

Map **9**

Detail from *The Declaration of Independence, July 4, 1776*. John Trumbull, 1819

The committee assigned to draft the Declaration of Independence in 1776 presents the document to John Hancock, president of the Continental Congress in Philadelphia. Shown in this detail from Trumbull's historical painting are (left to right) John Adams, Roger Sherman, Robert R. Livingston, Thomas Jefferson, and ßenjamin Franklin.

CHAPTER ONE

A Natural Genius for Art

[My] taste for drawing began to dawn early [and]
for several years [the] floors were constantly
scrawled with my rude attempts.
—*John Trumbull*

Nineteen-year-old Charlie Loring Elliott was full of hope when he visited the New York City studio of America's most famous artist in 1830. Elliott had come from western New York State to ask Colonel John Trumbull to accept him as a pupil in portrait painting.

Colonel Trumbull was a handsome, dignified gentleman in his seventies. He was a former officer in the Revolutionary War with fine manners and an old-fashioned formality. The Colonel, as he was known, had painted a number of the nation's most famous pictures. These were scenes from the American Revolution of more than forty-five years before.

Four of those paintings hung in the Capitol in Washington, D.C. The Colonel's works told the story of the founding of the United States. Shown in his pictures were individuals he had personally known, although by 1830 most of them had passed away and were only names in history books. They included John Adams, Thomas Jefferson, James Monroe, the Marquis de Lafayette, and General George Washington himself.

The son of a wealthy colonial governor, John Trumbull had been brought up like an aristocrat and had once associated with European royalty. By the 1830s, however, his world had changed, as had popular taste in the arts. The elderly Colonel was considered out of touch with current American art and artists. Still, he was much admired for all he had done in his life.

Trumbull looked over Elliott's drawings and his two oil paintings. Elliott knew young artists seldom received encouragement from Colonel Trumbull, who was president of the American Academy of Fine Arts. As he studied the pictures, the Colonel was most interested in designs for buildings Elliott had done for his father's architectural firm at home.

At last, Trumbull spoke. He strongly advised Elliott to give up painting and continue with architecture. Elliott was disappointed to hear Trumbull declare that being an artist was too uncertain a profession. The Colonel said it was difficult even for him to earn a living, despite his fifty-year career. "I have, it is true, received some commissions from Congress for national pictures," he continued, "but this was only a piece of good luck."

Although he had been successful in America and Europe, Trumbull was unable to sell much work in his later years. There was little public interest in his paintings anymore. "I am now an old man, and time and disappointment have chilled my ambition," he said sadly, as he gestured to the paintings on his walls. "Now, I must see if I have friends enough in the world to give these pictures to."

Elliott was not willing to admit defeat. Trumbull tried to change Elliott's mind, especially because the young man's architectural designs were so well done, but Elliott respectfully insisted that he did not want to be an architect. He said he was "fully determined, and have been ever since [I] was ten years old, to be a painter, and live or die by that business."

Perhaps the Colonel then remembered his own youthful determination to take his chances as an artist. Trumbull's parents also had objected at first. Finally, Elliott won him over, and Trumbull accepted him as a pupil.

After months of study, Elliott had made good progress. Still, the Colonel thought he should be an architect, and for very practical reasons: For one thing, Elliott was a superior architectural draftsman, a skill needed in a growing country.

In time, Elliott went to study with another artist who was more encouraging. Finally, unable to make a living, he could no longer remain in New York. Taking Colonel Trumbull's advice, he returned home to resume architectural design. Yet Elliott continued to paint, and his work began to attract patrons. His hope renewed, the aspiring artist went back to New York City, but he did not immediately visit Trumbull.

One day, the Colonel was strolling past a shop window and stopped to admire two paintings on exhibit. One was of a mounted soldier, and the other was an interior scene from an old New York household.

"Who painted these pictures?" he asked the shopkeeper.

"Elliott, Colonel Trumbull."

"Where is his room?"

Trumbull hurried there and knocked on the door. Removing his hat and entering, he bowed "with all the stateliness of the last century," Elliott remembered.

"You can go on painting, Sir," Trumbull said. "You need not follow architecture." With that, he bowed once more, saying, "I wish you good day, Sir," and left.

Elliott never saw him again, but that simple, direct assurance from the respected Colonel Trumbull meant the world to him.

In the following years, Elliott became New York's leading portrait painter. His clients were among the wealthiest and most successful people in the United States. Elliott remained a lifelong admirer of Trumbull, who finally did find the right home for his many paintings.

Remembering Trumbull some years after his death, Elliott told a journalist, "I owe much to the good old man, and I shall always be proud to say so."

All America eventually came to admire the works of Colonel John Trumbull, whose paintings show the founders of the United States in their finest hour.

A Connecticut Aristocrat

John Trumbull lived from 1756 to 1843. His lifetime of eighty-seven years began in colonial times and ended in the fast-growing young United States of America.

Trumbull was born into a merchant family in Lebanon, Connecticut. The Trumbulls bought and sold goods such as tea and rum. During the British colonial period, they often were called on to play a role as leaders in Connecticut and New England. In 1769, Trumbull's father, Jonathan, was named governor of Connecticut by King George III, ruler of the British Empire.

Great Britain was one of the world's most powerful nations, with possessions all around the globe. The empire's American colonies were among its richest—and also its most troublesome. When John Trumbull was a boy, many Americans wanted freedom from British colonial rule.

Jack, as they called him then, was the youngest of six children. Like most New Englanders, his family valued education. They enrolled their son in a private school just "three minutes' walk across a beautiful green," Trumbull later recalled in a memoir. It was, he said, the "best school in New England." Students came from all over the colonies to study with headmaster Nathan Tisdale, the instructor there for thirty years.

Young Jack was a brilliant student, who showed a special talent for languages. As he remembered, "I could read Greek at six years old." He taught himself French by

As a young artist, Trumbull often painted close members of his family, as in this 1777 canvas portraying his brother Jonathan with his wife and daughter. A basket of fruit, traditionally symbolizing fertility, was often included in New England paintings of women.

making friends with a French Canadian family that had moved into the community.

Yet drawing was what he loved best: "[A]fter school hours [I] frequently withdrew to my own room for a close study of my favorite pursuit." He said, "[My] taste for drawing began to dawn early [and] for several years [the] floors were constantly scrawled with my rude attempts." Although a fall down stairs caused him to lose the sight in his left eye, John became skilled at sketching pictures.

Choosing a Career

By the time he was fifteen, John's education at Tisdale's was complete. His father wanted him to enter Harvard College in Cambridge (near Boston) and become a minister or lawyer—the most highly respected careers in New England. Instead, his son asked to study art with Boston painter John Singleton Copley. John Trumbull admired Copley, whose work had thrilled him. Governor Trumbull agreed that his son had a "natural genius" for "limning," as painting was called, but the governor thought art was useless as a career.

John protested, saying that even after "the expense of a college education . . . I should still have to study some profession." He argued that if he studied art with Copley, he would possess a profession and the means of supporting himself. The governor firmly refused. John would attend Harvard.

Trumbull passed the entry exams with flying colors. He skipped the first two years and immediately joined the junior class. He was one of the youngest, and brightest, students in his class of thirty-six young men. While attending to his studies, he used any spare moments he could find to practice drawing and painting.

In Harvard's library he found illustrated books with engravings—black and white copies—of important European paintings. He studied those, as well as the artwork that hung on the college's walls. Trumbull made his own copies of the pictures and tried to learn how they were done. His copies included a picture of the eruption of the Italian volcano Mount Vesuvius and portraits of famous scientists and philosophers. He also copied a Copley portrait. Trumbull first attempted to paint in color when he was sixteen and copied his family's coat of arms.

Then he managed to meet Copley himself. In 1772, Trumbull's older brother Jonathan took him to the artist's elegant mansion in Boston. Copley was doing very well as a portrait painter, contrary to Governor Trumbull's opinion that artists could not make much of a living. Trumbull was very impressed by Copley, who was seventeen years older than he: "We found Mr. Copley dressed to receive a party of friends at dinner. [He was] an elegant looking man, dressed in fine maroon cloth, with gilt buttons—this was dazzling to [me]!"

During his own career, Trumbull would be well known for his elegant taste in clothes. He was always dashingly "turned out," even though his style eventually become rather old-fashioned for the times.

Seeing Copley and his paintings further inspired the sixteen-year-old Trumbull. They "absorbed my attention, and renewed all my desire to enter upon such a pursuit." Trumbull and Copley began a long friendship.

Meanwhile, Trumbull continued improving as an artist and found a few clients of his own. He sold an oil painting of a religious subject to his brother Jonathan for ten dollars—a good sum, considering that a working man earned just a few pennies a day.

Opposite: The Battle of Lexington. William Barnes Wollen, 1910

The Storm Breaks

After graduating from Harvard in 1773, Trumbull returned home to Lebanon, where he continued to study art. He did his own portrait several times and painted an original version of the Battle of Cannae, a famous incident from Roman times.

Even though John Trumbull painted several handsome portraits of his parents and brothers, Governor Trumbull was more impressed with his son's ability in languages. The governor especially appreciated that he had not had to pay a tutor—his son had learned French on his own. When Nathan Tisdale fell ill that year, Trumbull temporarily took over as headmaster at the private school, teaching as many as eighty pupils.

By now, troubles between Great Britain and its American colonies were growing worse, especially in New England. The crisis was brought to a head that year by the Boston Tea Party, in which rebellious Americans threw tea on British ships into the harbor rather than pay a tax on it. As punishment, the British government shut down Boston's trade and commerce, which made many colonials even angrier. Unrest in Boston was so troubling that in 1774 Copley left for London. In England, life was more peaceful, and there were many wealthy art patrons who wanted their portraits painted.

All over America, young men were joining militia companies to resist British oppression. John Trumbull helped organize a local company of militia to be prepared

John Singleton Copley was the portraitist who inspired the younger Trumbull to paint and became his lifelong friend.

Self-Portrait. John Singleton Copley, 1780–1784

The Patriots fired at a wall of Redcoats just as the sun was rising at Lexington. Poet Ralph Waldo Emerson described the first shot, which heralded the start of the American Revolution, as the "shot heard 'round the world."

in case open conflict erupted with government troops—called "Redcoats," for the color of their uniforms.

The whole of British America was shocked in April 1775, when New England militia attacked and defeated a powerful force of Redcoats near Boston. Thousands of militia, including Trumbull's own company, turned out for these battles of Lexington and Concord. He marched to Boston and joined the siege of the Redcoats who were occupying the city. This uprising was, as Trumbull wrote, "The tempest which had long been preparing."

This detail from *The Surrender of Lord Cornwallis at Yorktown* shows the tremendous care Trumbull gave to portray accurate scenes. Each of these Patriot officers has recognizable features, a unique expression, and a perfectly rendered uniform depicting his rank.

CHAPTER TWO

The Patriot Colonel

I now suddenly found myself in the family of one of the most distinguished and dignified men of the age.
—John Trumbull, serving George Washington

In the 1775 siege of Boston, John Trumbull joined the First Connecticut Regiment as adjutant-assistant to the regimental commander. Like other junior Revolutionary officers, Trumbull proudly wore a cockade of folded green ribbon on his hat.

That June, he watched through a field telescope as British troops stormed and captured American defenses in a bloody clash known as the Battle of Bunker (or Bunker's) Hill. More than 1,000 British and 400 Americans were casualties that day. The fierceness of the battle appalled both sides.

At the time, Trumbull's sister, Faith, was visiting the Patriot camp to see her husband, a militia commander. When she witnessed the horrors of battle, Faith was terrified to think what her husband and brother would face in the coming struggle. Trumbull's memoir described her situation: "She found herself surrounded not by the 'pomp and circumstance of glorious war,' but in the midst of all its horrible realities. [I]t overcame her strong, but too sensitive mind. She became deranged, and died the following November."

In that troubled summer of 1775, few Americans could imagine the misery and sorrow of the coming eight years. The Revolutionary War would tear apart the once prosperous and peaceful colonies. Families would become divided, as members chose between rebellion and loyalty to the king. What began as a revolution against British rule turned into a civil war.

Trumbull was with the Revolutionary army soon after the Battle of Bunker Hill, when George Washington arrived to take command. The general was impressed by drawings of the British defensive positions Trumbull had done. Trumbull had been aware that Washington "was very desirous of obtaining a correct plan of the enemy's works." He had risked his life by creeping out through long grass to spy on the British. He was invited to join Washington's staff as an aide. Already his artistic skill was proving of great value.

Trumbull became part of Washington's "military family," with duties that included receiving important military and civilian guests. He came to greatly admire Washington. "I now suddenly found myself," Trumbull wrote, "in the family of one of the most distinguished and dignified men of the age."

His Excellency, as the general was called, and Trumbull were both refined gentlemen. Like Trumbull, Washington was extremely conscious of his appearance and was always perfectly dressed. The young aide was well suited to his duties, having grown up in a governor's home, where he often met New England officials. Important people came

Opposite: Detail from The Death of General Mercer at the Battle of Princeton, January 3, 1777. *John Trumbull, c. 1789*

Study for The Death of General Warren at the Battle of Bunker's Hill, June 17, 1775. *John Trumbull, 1786*

This is one of several charcoal and wash studies for Trumbull's *The Death of General Warren at the Battle of Bunker's Hill.* The sketch shows the artist's final choices for light and dark areas, and the positioning of the principal subjects, including Patriot leader, Dr. Joseph Warren (center), lying near death.

The much-admired Patriot general Hugh Mercer is shown about to be killed in this detail from Trumbull's *The Death of General Mercer at the Battle of Princeton*. Washington, mounted, leads the Revolutionary forces in this crucial 1777 victory.

to Washington's headquarters to discuss the widening war. Trumbull met the new nation's present and future leaders—in his own words, "the first people of the country"—who would prove helpful to him in his future career.

In time, though, Trumbull felt "unequal to the elegant duties of my situation." He preferred a field command to running the busy headquarters. It was a relief when Washington brought two fellow Virginians into the household as aides. Trumbull then became a brigade commander, with the rank of major.

The siege of Boston continued until March 1776, when the British abandoned the city. To the immense joy of the Patriot forces, the British navy's fleet carried the soldiers away without further fighting. The siege of Boston was one of Washington's finest victories, achieved with almost no bloodshed, a welcome contrast to the 1775 Battle of

This detail from Trumbull's historical painting, *The Death of General Montgomery in the Attack on Quebec,* portrays the moment Montgomery died in the arms of his officers. The American commander has been hit by cannon fire from Loyalist and British defenders of the city in 1775.

Bunker Hill. Trumbull would always remember that savage battle, and he intended to paint a picture of it.

Colonel Trumbull

Trumbull was promoted to the rank of colonel, although he was just twenty years old. He was entitled to wear the red cockade that signified his higher rank. By the summer of 1776, he was stationed at Fort Ticonderoga, the main strongpoint on the inland water route between Canada and New York. He was a staff officer to General Horatio Gates, whose force was positioned to support a Patriot invasion of Canada.

That summer, Trumbull witnessed the sudden retreat of the invasion force, which had been defeated. A stream of sick and wounded soldiers arrived at Ticonderoga in rowboats and canoes. He said that it was difficult to imagine men being any more miserable than the "wretched remnant" that survived. They had only half-cooked salt pork and hard crackers to eat, and there was no medicine for their fevers and wounds. "The boats were leaky and without awnings," he wrote, "the sick being laid upon their bottoms without straw were soon drenched in the filthy water, [and] exposed to the burning sun."

It was Trumbull's sad duty to examine the defeated troops and account for the wounded. They were sheltered in sheds and tents and under huts made of bushes. He wrote, "I can truly say that I did not look into a tent or hut in which I did not find a dead or dying man."

The Patriot triumph at Boston was now a distant memory. Not only had the invasion of Canada been a disaster, but Washington's main army had been defeated at New York. Everywhere, the Patriots seemed to be in retreat. Also, a powerful British force was moving south from Canada to attack Fort Ticonderoga.

Trumbull worked with military engineers to strengthen the fort's defenses. He warned the commanders that Patriot forces must fortify Mount Defiance, a rocky bluff that overlooked Ticonderoga. He explained to them that if British cannons were placed on the bluff, the British could bombard the fort, which would have to be abandoned.

The Patriot commanders did not believe artillery could be pulled up the steep mountainside. To prove his point, Trumbull and several officers hauled a cannon to the top of Mount Defiance. He even had Patriot cannoneers in the fort try to fire at the top of Defiance, but their cannonballs could not reach it. Despite his efforts, Trumbull's advice was ignored, and Mount Defiance remained unfortified.

Trumbull was an active and efficient staff officer. His rank of colonel was only temporary, however, and had to be officially confirmed by Congress. He wrote to members of Congress in Philadelphia, requesting this confirmation, but months passed with no reply. By late summer, Trumbull was furious at being ignored. He wrote to his brother, "My commission is not receiv'd yet—I look on myself as insulted."

Despite his resentment of the lack of response from Congress, Trumbull kept working hard at Fort Ticonderoga. The Patriot force awaited the British, who were building a powerful fleet to carry their army down Lake Champlain.

Triumph and Insult

That expected enemy attack was delayed by a courageous but doomed Patriot flotilla of small vessels that engaged the British warships on the lake. Led by another Connecticut native, General Benedict Arnold, the Patriot boats helped slow the enemy invasion. By the time the British fleet arrived at Ticonderoga, it was October, and cold weather was setting in. When the British fleet anchored a few miles away, every Patriot soldier in the fort was armed, and every flag and banner was flying. Although there was no time for painting or drawing, Trumbull's artist's eye took in the spectacle.

Ticonderoga must have looked imposing that day when viewed from the lake. The

Trumbull came to know many of America's Revolutionary leaders, as well as British and French notables of his day. None influenced him as powerfully as George Washington.

Many of Washington's young officers were in awe of him and loved him like a father. Trumbull expressed his admiration by painting Washington's portrait several times. He completed the first great military portrait in 1782, when he was serving as a military supply contractor to the general's army in New York's Hudson Valley. He did the second portrait, which commemorated the 1776 victory at Trenton, in 1792, when Washington was president.

In preparation for the Trenton portrait, Trumbull and Washington discussed the desperate and dangerous plan of attack in 1776. Washington took on a worried look as he recalled those days. Trumbull "happily transferred to the canvass [that look of] high resolve to conquer or to perish."

Trumbull's portrait *General George Washington at Trenton* conveys the artist's admiration for the revolutionary commander whom he once served as aide-de-camp. The 1776 victory at Trenton saved the Patriot army to fight another day.

General George Washington at Trenton. John Trumbull, 1792

hills on both sides of the lake were crowned with defensive barriers and artillary units, all manned, and a splendid show of artillery and flags.

The British did not want to risk having their army caught outdoors in northern New York's harsh winter. They withdrew south across Lake Champlain, intending to renew the invasion that spring. Once again, Trumbull was part of a Patriot triumph—if only a temporary one.

Soon, Trumbull and Arnold left Fort Ticonderoga to join Washington, who had withdrawn to near Philadelphia. It was almost Christmas, and Washington was planning a daring counterattack against an enemy force that held Trenton, New Jersey. Trumbull and Arnold would not be part of this coming victory, though. Instead, they were ordered to Rhode Island to oppose British troops who had captured Newport.

A Point of Pride

Early in 1777, Congress officially approved Trumbull's commission as a colonel, but he was unhappy when he read the confirming papers. The commission was dated ten weeks later than the date of his original promotion. The official date of a commission determined an officer's seniority: colonels with an earlier commission date would rank higher than Trumbull.

Always committed to proper formality, Trumbull refused to accept this injustice. He wrote to John Hancock, president of Congress, to request that his commission be dated correctly. Again, he received no reply.

Frustrated and insulted by this lack of consideration, Trumbull resigned from the Revolutionary army after a year and a half of service. He wrote a Massachusetts delegate to Congress:

> I should have less reason to complain, did I not know that officers [who had been] inferior in rank to myself, have been advanced and commissioned without the least difficulty. . . . From this day, therefore, I lay aside my cockade and sword, with the fixed determination never to resume them until I can do it with honor.

Disappointed and resentful, Trumbull returned to Lebanon and resumed his painting: "Thus ended my regular military service, to my deep regret, for my mind was at this time full of lofty military aspirations."

At least Trumbull would now have the time for painting, which he had neglected all these months while serving in the military. Still, his rank of colonel in the Revolutionary army would always be a point of pride for him.

Self-Portrait. John Trumbull, c. 1802

Trumbull was in his mid-forties and at the height of his artistic powers when he painted this self-portrait. He was living in England, recently married, and planning to return to the United States. The sword, paintbrushes, and his cultured appearance portray Trumbull as an artist, patriot soldier, and gentleman.

CHAPTER THREE

An American Artist

The sound of the drum frequently called an
involuntary tear to my eye.
—John Trumbull, after leaving military service

The Revolutionary War erupted in several major battles during 1777. The civilian John Trumbull followed the conflict through news that reached his home in Lebanon, Connecticut.

In northern New York, a powerful British army captured Fort Ticonderoga, which the Patriots had abandoned without a fight. The British commander, General John Burgoyne, had discovered the fort's weakness. As Trumbull had warned, Mount Defiance had become occupied by the enemy and after that Ticonderoga was doomed.

The fort fell in the summer, and violence raged through the northern frontier. Native American warriors and Loyalists, who supported the king, attacked Patriot settlements and farms, leaving many in ruins. The suffering people of northern New York called 1777 "The Year of the Bloody Sevens."

The British army defeated Washington in battle and captured Philadelphia. Congress fled the city. Washington counterattacked, but his forces were driven back. Meanwhile, British general Burgoyne advanced down the Hudson River and was threatening Albany. It was possible that he might still turn eastward and move against New England.

Trumbull worried about Burgoyne's invasion as he observed events from Lebanon. "A deep . . . regret of the military career from which I had been driven, and to which there appeared to be no possibility of an honorable return, preyed upon my spirits; and the sound of the drum frequently called an involuntary tear to my eye."

Lithograph of *Spirit of '76*, Archibald M. Willard, 1876

Nineteenth-century American artist Archibald M. Willard painted several versions of this *Spirit of '76*, which became famous imagery celebrating the Patriot spirit of the American Revolution.

Torn Between Painter and Patriot

Trumbull kept busy painting portraits of friends and family, including himself. He continued to copy paintings hanging on walls and illustrations in books. His family was still unconvinced that art could be a successful career. They wanted him to join the family business. Instead, Trumbull longed to go to Boston, even though his friend Copley had moved to England.

Many American-born artists were living in London and were recognized as among the best in the empire. They were led by Pennsylvanian Benjamin West, one of the finest painters of the day. Copley was working in West's studio and already had achieved success in London.

West was teaching young American artists who had left their home country to be his pupils. He had been living in Europe since 1760—first in Rome and, by 1763, in England. West had won an enthusiastic following among Britain's wealthy, and he was named "historical painter" to King George III in 1772.

Trumbull was especially drawn to West's historical paintings, which showed scenes from important events, including some from America. These were the kinds of pictures Trumbull most loved to paint.

One of West's best-known works was *The Death of General Wolfe.* This was a painting of the famed British commander's final moments, after he was wounded while capturing Quebec from the French in 1759. All of French Canada had fallen to the British by 1763.

Now, almost fifteen years later, Canada was key to British military operations against the American Revolutionaries. This colony did not join in the American Revolution. Instead, Canada was dominated by Loyalists, who favored the British. Canada was the supply base for Burgoyne's army as it marched south toward Albany. Burgoyne's hopes for triumph were dashed, however, when he was surrounded at Saratoga by a Patriot army under Gates and utterly defeated.

France now entered the struggle on the Patriot side. Within a few months, the tide had turned in favor of the revolutionaries.

A Studio in Boston

Restless, Trumbull finally moved to Boston at the close of 1777. There, he joined a club of young men who had recently graduated from Harvard College. They were, as Trumbull put it, "men who in after life became distinguished."

They included Rufus King, a future New York senator who helped to write, or "frame," the federal Constitution; Christopher Gore, a future Massachusetts governor; and Royal Tyler, who would become a successful playwright and a judge. One friend would become secretary of war, another a foreign minister, and others would be important legal thinkers and professors. Trumbull painted several of their portraits.

This lively group would gather at Trumbull's room on Queen Street, near the State House. His studio had once belonged to John Smibert, whom Trumbull described as "the patriarch of painting in America." Born in Scotland, Smibert had settled in Boston in 1730, where he worked as a portrait painter and teacher and earned the title of "Father of American painting."

Smibert had died in 1751, leaving behind several paintings that were his copies of Old Masters (as the best painters from previous centuries were called). Although Trumbull regretted that there was no accomplished artist in Boston "from whom I could gain oral instruction," he found "several copies by [Smibert] from celebrated pictures in Europe, which were very useful to me."

So Trumbull studied and copied Smibert's own copies of works by such renowned artists as Flemish painter Sir Anthony Van Dyck, French artist Nicholas Poussin, and Italian painter Raphael. Then, in mid-1778, the war flared up again, and Trumbull volunteered to return to the army.

A Conspicuous Target

The Patriots and their French allies were planning to drive the British from Newport, Rhode Island. Trumbull heard that a French fleet had arrived off New York to prepare for the campaign. The Americans would be led by General John Sullivan, whom Trumbull knew from the Canadian invasion. He decided to join him: "I seized this occasion to gratify my slumbering love of military life, and offered my services to General Sullivan as a volunteer aide-de-camp. My offer was accepted and I attended him during the enterprise."

That "enterprise" did not succeed, for the French fleet was battered by a storm and forced to withdraw. Sullivan did not have the numbers to attack the British force in Newport, which could be supplied and reinforced by its own fleet. The Patriot army had to withdraw, and Trumbull was sent to alert the troops. He was soon in danger as the enemy counterattacked.

Trumbull rode on horseback near the battlefront as enemy cannon fired. He was an easy target, because he wore light-colored civilian clothes with a white handkerchief tied around his head to replace the hat blown away by the wind: "Grape shot [small but deadly lead balls] began to sprinkle around me, and soon after musket balls fell in my path like hailstones. I formed . . . the most conspicuous mark that ever was seen on the field—mounted on a superb bay horse . . . with this head-dress, duty led me to every

The Surrender of General Burgoyne at Saratoga, October 16, 1777. John Trumbull, c. 1822

The British Empire was stunned when the army of General John Burgoyne, with sword at center-left, was captured by the Patriots during the New York campaign of 1777. Trumbull's *The Surrender of General Burgoyne at Saratoga* is one of the paintings exhibited at the Capitol Rotunda in Washington, D.C.

point where danger was to be found, and I escaped without the slightest injury."

During one engagement, Trumbull watched a force of enemy troops retreat, although the overmatched Patriot army would eventually withdraw from the battle. He advanced and found an officer's sword, which he kept as a trophy to remember this moment after returning to Lebanon and civilian life once more.

Once back home, Trumbull was persuaded to enter the family mercantile business. He was unhappy, however, for he remained determined to be an artist. Within a few months, he was back in Boston.

A Need to Study in Europe

Trumbull's Boston paintings included copies of other artists' pictures. One was a portrait of Patriot leader Benjamin Franklin, based on a French engraving that showed the statesman in a fur cap. Trumbull also copied a portrait of George Washington by Charles Willson Peale, the leading Philadelphia portraitist.

By now, Trumbull was eager to go to London and study with Benjamin West. This was the best way to further his progress as an artist. However, a former Patriot soldier, such as Trumbull, would be permitted to come to London only if he did not get involved in politics. It helped that he knew so many important people—some with "high connections in England."

One of his distinguished friends, also a friend of West's, urged Trumbull to come and study with him. This man was considered neutral in the Revolution and had close friends at the top levels of the British government. With his help, Trumbull was given official permission to come to England.

Although many colonials were in revolt against the mother country, there was still much mercantile business between Britain and America. Trumbull was asked by some friends to represent them in Europe, where they hoped to arrange for foreign investment in American commercial projects. If Trumbull was successful in this enterprise, he would share in the profits.

TRUMBULL'S PAINTING METHODS

As a young painter teaching himself, Trumbull valued the words of English historical painter William Hogarth. In a 1777 self-portrait, Trumbull's neatly prepared palette and colors rest on Hogarth's 1753 book, *Analysis of Beauty*. In an 1812 self-portrait, his colors are laid out in accord with Hogarth's color scheme: flake white, Naples yellow, Venetian red, vermilion, raw umber, and blue black.

Trumbull's main influence was Benjamin West, who urged artists to use opposite colors next to each other. This means red next to green, blue next to orange, yellow beside purple. This, said West, "is the fundamental principle from which Harmony & Brilliance of Colour results."

West also suggested coating a color with a transparent glaze made of the opposite color. This will "at once reduce the Colour to the depth requir'd & at the same time give the most pleasing Modesty & Union of tone."

This portrait of Benjamin Franklin shows the famous Patriot diplomat in plain clothing, but with a handsome and very costly fur hat. The painting was copied from an engraving Trumbull saw while he was in Connecticut.

Benjamin Franklin.
John Trumbull, 1778

Trumbull decided to go to Paris first and then travel through the Netherlands to reach England. Hearing of his plans, Benjamin Franklin offered Trumbull a position as secretary, to work for him in Europe. Trumbull declined, worried that such duties might not allow him the time to pursue an artistic career. Still, Franklin wrote him a letter of introduction to West.

Trumbull left for Europe in May 1780. The ongoing war was behind him now, or so he thought. Once in Paris, he became involved in legitimate business affairs, but several British officials suspected he was on a secret mission.

Benjamin Franklin arrived back in France about the same time as Trumbull. Some historians suggest that Trumbull was actually a spy for Franklin, but we do not know for certain. He never revealed the truth, one way or the other.

Trumbull loved France, where his ability to speak the language made it easy to make friends. His business matters were unsuccessful, however, partly because the American War, as it was known, was now going against the Patriots. Few Europeans wanted to risk investing with Americans, who seemed to be backing a lost cause. At the first opportunity, Trumbull left the Continent for London and the studio of Benjamin West.

The American School. Matthew Pratt, 1765

American artist Matthew Pratt painted *The American School* in 1765, depicting the London studio of Benjamin West. As West gives a critique at left, Pratt sits at far right, holding a palette, paintbrush, and maulstick (to rest his hand on while he painted). The other figures are not identified.

CHAPTER FOUR

Studio and Prison

Mr. Trumbull, I have now no hesitation to say that
nature intended you for a painter.
—*Benjamin West*

Immediately after arriving in London in July 1780, Trumbull made sure to inform the authorities that he was in the country. He hoped to avoid any further suspicion about his intentions. That was not to be, though. Thousands of Loyalists lived in Britain, having fled America after losing all they owned because they opposed the Revolution. Some Loyalists, who were politically powerful, called for Trumbull's arrest. Since he had taken arms in America against the king, they said, he should be charged with treason.

Trumbull knew that West was admired and influential in Britain. If Trumbull was accepted as a pupil of the king's historical painter, it surely would mean a successful future for the young artist. At least, the Loyalists might stop calling for his arrest.

Trumbull was "most kindly received" at West's studio—his "painting-room"—where many handsome pictures hung on the walls. In the adjoining rooms, student artists and assistants were busily working.

West was in his mid-forties, well-dressed and straightforward. Like Trumbull, he was largely self-taught, though he had studied for a while with an accomplished British artist who had immigrated to Pennsylvania. As a boy back in Pennsylvania, West had learned about paint from local Indians. They had taught him to mix colors in a pot, using river clay and bear grease.

Trumbull was well educated, while West had little formal education and could barely spell. Yet he had founded the Royal Academy of Arts and painted members of the royal family and King George III (twice). Few artists had more stature than Benjamin West.

Now West came right to the point and asked whether this ambitious Connecticut newcomer had brought examples of his work to show. Trumbull had not. "Then look around the room," West said, "and see if there is anything you would like to copy." Trumbull examined the works and selected a beautiful round picture of a mother and two children.

"West looked keenly at me," Trumbull said. He asked, "'Do you know what you have chosen?' 'No, sir.' 'That, Mr. Trumbull, is called the Madonna della Sedia, the Madonna of the chair, one of the most admired works of Raphael; the selection of such a work is a good omen.'"

The master took the pupil into another room to introduce him to "a young countryman of ours who is studying with me—he will show you where to find the necessary colors, tools, etc., and you will make your copy in the same room."

So began Trumbull's lifelong friendship with fellow New Englander Gilbert Stuart. A native of Rhode Island, Stuart was a successful portraitist. He and Trumbull got off to a good start in West's studio, where Trumbull was happily reunited with John Singleton Copley.

After some weeks, when Trumbull's copy was finished, West "carefully examined and compared it." Then he said, "Mr. Trumbull, I have now no hesitation to say that nature intended you for a painter." All that was needed now, West said, was serious work and study.

With that encouragement, wrote Trumbull, "[I] devoted myself . . . to the study of the art, allowing myself little time to make myself acquainted with the curiosities and amusements of the city." But if this serious young painter paid little attention to the world around him, the same could not be said about the world. It was well aware of his presence.

The Patriot in Prison

Revolutionary America went through a major crisis in 1780. Leading Patriot General Benedict Arnold turned traitor and joined the British and Loyalists. Arnold's co-conspirator, a young Redcoat officer named John André, was captured, tried, and hanged as a spy.

The execution of the much-admired André caused a storm of anger in Britain. There were calls for the execution of a Patriot in revenge. Colonel John Trumbull seemed a perfect candidate.

Trumbull's career was stopped short in November 1780, when he was arrested and charged with bearing arms against the king. "A thunderbolt falling at my feet, would not have been more astounding," he said, "for . . . I had become as confident of safety in London, as I should have been in Lebanon."

Trumbull was proud of his Revolutionary service and showed no regrets, even though it might mean his execution. He was taken to prison, well aware that angry mobs from time to time stormed jails and murdered prisoners. As a man of some wealth, he was permitted to choose his place of detention, as long as he could pay for his own upkeep.

That choice was Tothill Fields Bridewell, an old building with a high wall and a pretty garden. He had his own room, "neatly furnished," and during the day was free to use the garden. There he waited while West and other friends tried to win his release. As months passed, it became clear that the government would not execute him, since doing so might spur the Patriots to execute a British prisoner in return. In addition, King George gave West the "royal promise, that [Trumbull's] life shall be safe."

Trumbull was visited by West and others, and also by several leading British statesmen who opposed the American War. These included Members of Parliament Edmund Burke and Charles J. Fox, who also were working for his release. In spite of all the sympathy for Trumbull, even the king refused to interfere. There was too much anger on the British side against the revolutionaries. To make matters worse for Trumbull during this time, his mother passed away in Connecticut.

In prison, Trumbull copied pictures provided by West, and sometimes he used fellow inmates as models. He also spent time studying books on architecture, which began to appeal to him strongly.

Some of his work from prison was exhibited at the Royal Academy, where the pictures were admired. It was not generally known that they had been done in "the gloom of a prison," said Horace Walpole, a leading English politician.

At last, after Trumbull had endured seven long months in Bridewell, the efforts of some of Britain's most influential politicians were successful. King George finally ordered him released, "with the condition," said Trumbull, "that I should leave the kingdom within thirty days, and not return until after peace had been restored."

Home to Lebanon

Trumbull set off for the Continent to find a ship for his passage to America. His health had suffered during his confinement, and he was bitter at losing the opportunity to learn from Benjamin West. It was now June 1781, and the allied Patriots and

THE "AMERICAN SCHOOL" IN LONDON

When Trumbull first arrived in London in 1780, he hoped to study with Benjamin West for two years and then spend a year in Rome. The Rome study was not to be, but West offered Trumbull all he could have wanted as a student.

West arranged a demanding course of study for him which included drawing classes at the Royal Academy. This was a dream come true for Trumbull, who had spent so many lonely hours teaching himself by copying old paintings. Now, there were instructors to guide him and fellow students to talk to about art. And there was stimulating competition among the students, who were some of the finest young artists in the country.

Trumbull wrote home that he was, "among boys, some of whom draw better than I do:—but I have the pleasure to find that my labor is not in vain, & to hear Judges of the Art declare that I have made a more rapid progress . . . than they have before known."

Among the American artists in West's London studio—the "American School," they were called—were Charles Willson Peale, Ralph Earl, Matthew Pratt, John Singleton Copley, Gilbert Stuart, William Dunlap, Washington Allston, Thomas Sully, and Samuel F.B. Morse. These men were accomplished portraitists, many of whom would become the leading American artists of the nineteenth century.

Dunlap later wrote about West's generosity as a teacher: "He had no secrets or mysteries, he told all he knew." Benjamin West was president of the Royal Academy of Arts almost continuously from 1792 until his death in 1820.

Gilbert Stuart. Benjamin West, 1781

Rhode Islander Gilbert Stuart was a protégé of Benjamin West, who painted his portrait in 1781. Stuart had great success after emigrating to London, where his work brought some of the highest prices in Britain. He returned to America in 1793 and continued painting until his death in Boston in 1828.

French were moving against a British army under Lord Charles Cornwallis at Yorktown, Virginia.

Trumbull's ocean journey, which finally began in France in mid-August, was long and dangerous, with unfavorable winds and stormy seas. He had to change ships in Spain, and his vessel was always at risk of meeting British warships. Trumbull at last saw the hills around Boston "in the afternoon of a beautiful day in January" 1782.

During his journey, Trumbull had learned of the great victory by Washington and the French at Yorktown in November. The Revolutionary War was drawing to a close, and the former thirteen colonies would soon become independent states.

"I returned to Lebanon as soon as possible," Trumbull recalled. "My reflections were painful—I had thrown away two of the most precious years of life [and] had encountered many dangers . . . to no purpose." The unhappy Trumbull fell seriously ill, and, for some time, he seemed near death. He did not recover until the fall of 1782, when he entered his brother Jonathan's business, supplying the Revolutionary Army.

Trumbull was glad to rejoin General Washington, who was at his military base in the Hudson Valley. The Patriots were waiting for the last British troops to leave New York City. In the meantime, Trumbull painted a full-length portrait of Washington, who was pleased to pose for his former aide.

After the British withdrew from New York City in December 1783, the war officially ended. Trumbull again faced the choice of a mercantile career or the life of an artist. He continued to struggle with his father, who still wanted him to study law. "I pined for the arts," he wrote in his memoir.

Arguing with his father, Trumbull "entered into an elaborate defense" of the arts. But his able arguments only convinced his father all the more that his son would make a fine lawyer. Trumbull replied by pointing to "the honors paid to artists in the glorious days of Greece and Athens." "You appear to forget, sir," Governor Trumbull replied, "that Connecticut is not Athens."

After that time, however, Trumbull's father never again argued with his son in favor of the law as a career. In 1784, at last receiving the governor's blessing, Trumbull returned to London to resume studying with Benjamin West.

The Capture of the Hessians at Trenton shows the surrender of the mortally wounded German commander (center left, supported by an American officer) to General Washington (center, on brown horse) on December 25, 1776. Trumbull narrowly missed being at this battle. He was instead on his way to New England, carrying out a mission for Washington.

CHAPTER FIVE

Portraying the Revolution's Finest Moments

To speak of its merit I can only say that in looking at it my whole frame contracted, my blood shivered, and I felt a faintness at my heart. He is the first painter who has undertaken by his pencil those great actions, that gave birth to our nation.
–Abigail Adams,
about Trumbull's painting of Bunker Hill

Back in London, Trumbull followed a "strict regimen, waking at five to study anatomy, breakfasting at eight, then painting all day." He was never happier than when employing "the pencil" and learning all he could about art.

West introduced him to many artists, writers, diplomats, and members of the aristocracy. Trumbull even had tea with Copley at Windsor Castle, one of the royal family's homes, where they strolled freely in the king's magnificent gardens.

Trumbull took classes at the Royal Academy and practiced his technical skills "with ardor." Yet he soon faced unexpected criticism, and it came from none other than England's most prominent portrait painter: Sir Joshua Reynolds, who was a good friend of West's.

While visiting the studio, Reynolds saw Trumbull's recent portrait of a prosperous Connecticut merchant. Trumbull recalled how, "in a quick sharp tone," Sir Joshua declared, "That coat is bad, sir, very bad." Reynolds scoffed that the coat "is not cloth—it is tin, bent tin."

Trumbull's pride was wounded. Still he kept learning and improving, always encouraged by the kindly West.

Images of Revolution

Trumbull's family missed him, especially his elderly, widower father. "His mind dwells much on his absent son," wrote his brother Jonathan, "and the longing Wish of his Heart is, that he may live to see him once more returned to his fond embraces." Yet Trumbull was too absorbed in his work to return home.

He began to paint his own historical pictures. Among these were revolutionary scenes from 1775: the Quebec siege of the Canadian campaign and Bunker Hill (or Bunker's) at Boston, which showed the death of Patriot leader General Joseph Warren, killed during the British assault.

Even before this second picture was finished, he received great praise from West, who invited him to join a number of "brother artists"—including Reynolds—for dinner at the studio. West made sure the Bunker Hill painting was the center of attention.

> [Reynolds] immediately ran up to my picture—'Why, West, what have you got here?'—'this is better colored than your works are generally.' 'Sir Joshua, (was the reply,) you mistake—that is not mine—it is the work of this young gentleman, Mr. Trumbull; permit me to introduce him to you.'

Trumbull thought Reynolds was at least as shocked then as he had been by Reynolds's "bent tin" criticism. More satisfying than that, West called the painting the "best picture" ever done of a modern battle.

Abigail Adams, the wife of Massachusetts diplomat John Adams, saw the painting in London and was emotionally shaken by it. She had lived through the siege of Boston and knew many of the people Trumbull pictured. She wrote to her sister:

> To speak of its merit I can only say that in looking at it my whole frame contracted, my blood shivered, and I felt a faintness at my heart. He is the first painter who has undertaken by his pencil those great actions, that gave birth to our nation.

Colonel John Trumbull was taking his rightful place among the most accomplished historical painters of the day. It was around this time that he resolved to paint a series of scenes from the Revolution. He wrote to Jonathan that he wished "to take up the History of Our Country, and paint the principal Events . . . of the late War."

West enthusiastically urged Trumbull to carry through with this series, especially since Trumbull had been a Revolutionary soldier and knew many of the participants. Encouragement also came from the American minister to France, Thomas Jefferson, who was visiting London. Jefferson was moved by Trumbull's painting of General Warren's death at the battle of Bunker Hill. In his memoir, Trumbull noted that Jefferson "invited me to come to Paris, to see and study the fine works there, and to make his house my home during my stay."

It was a momentous invitation, for Jefferson had many important friends in France—both artists and art collectors. No aspiring painter could have been offered a better opportunity to see firsthand the galleries of the Parisian elite. At the same time, however, came the sad news of Governor Trumbull's death. From London, thousands of miles across the sea, Trumbull could not go home to join his relatives in mourning the much-loved head of their family.

Art and Society in Paris

In summer 1786, Trumbull arrived in Paris, where Jefferson lived elegantly in the society of many leading people of the day. Jefferson introduced Trumbull to important French artists whose work he admired, including the sculptor Jean Antoine Houdon and the painter Jacques Louis David.

Trumbull also became friends with the English miniaturist Richard Cosway. Trumbull was himself an accomplished painter of miniatures—small portraits, usually a few inches square and placed in oval frames or lockets. He was fascinated by Cosway's work, calling him "the admired miniature painter of the day." Cosway's subjects included the most prominent personalities of France and Britain.

Cosway and his beautiful wife, Maria, who was also an artist, were close friends with Jefferson. They took Trumbull on delightful visits to the homes of aristocrats, palaces, splendid formal gardens, old churches and cathedrals, and even the private homes of royalty. There, he saw collections of paintings by the greatest of the Old Masters.

Paris was a breathtaking whirlwind of excitement and pleasure that summer. Refined and dignified, and fluent in French, Trumbull was an attractive newcomer to Parisian high society. The aristocratic French gave a warm reception to this Connecticut Yankee.

Some of his hosts had helped finance—and had even fought as officers in—the Revolutionary War, including the famed political figures the Marquis de Lafayette and the Comte de Vaudreuil. Both had been instrumental in winning French support of the Revolution, and Lafayette had been a key commander for Washington. Doors were open everywhere to the American soldier-painter, who was a friend of Jefferson and a

Preceding spread: Trumbull's paintings of the deaths of heroes are rich in drama and sentimental feeling. Here, American General Richard Montgomery has fallen, and General Benedict Arnold (right) rushes in to take command.

The Death of General Montgomery in the Attack on Quebec, December 31, 1775. John Trumbull, 1786

Trumbull painted this miniature of his friend Thomas Jefferson for English artist Maria Cosway in 1788. Trumbull had already done Jefferson's portrait in Paris the previous winter, and this is a copy. Trumbull considered it one of his best small portraits.

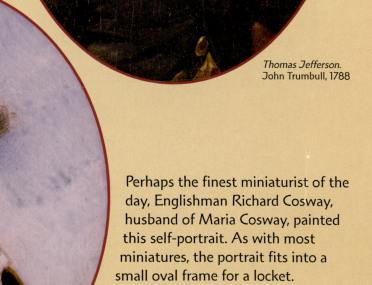

Thomas Jefferson.
John Trumbull, 1788

Perhaps the finest miniaturist of the day, Englishman Richard Cosway, husband of Maria Cosway, painted this self-portrait. As with most miniatures, the portrait fits into a small oval frame for a locket.

Self-portrait miniature (ivory).
Richard Cosway, date unknown

The Death of General Mercer at the Battle of Princeton, January 3, 1777. John Trumbull, c. 1789

The Patriot victory at Princeton, New Jersey, in 1777 allowed Washington to reorganize his forces and prove the rebellion was not yet defeated. The victory was bittersweet because of the loss of General Hugh Mercer.

rising star. His paintings of Bunker Hill and Quebec were warmly received in France.

Trumbull's work was generously praised by admirers, including the "Connoisseurs," as the leading French art patrons and critics were termed. Trumbull's personal guides included Houdon (later to sculpt Washington, Franklin, and Jefferson) and David, who had great influence on Trumbull's painting style. He even was shown the king's own collection at Versailles and at the royal family's gallery at Luxembourg Palace in Paris.

Trumbull was dismayed to see a sadly neglected collection of fabulous artwork in the Louvre, the former royal residence in the heart of Paris. He also toured the wonderful, but poorly cared for, art at the Royal Academy. Paris had such an abundance of art that the owners could not care for it all. Canvases were soiled, frames mildewed, and dust was allowed to collect on even the valuable work of Old Masters.

Trumbull not only saw paintings by many long-gone artists he so admired—among them the Flemish painter Peter Paul Rubens and Dutch painter Rembrandt—but he and Jefferson discussed how to paint the most important scenes of the Revolution. The first, they agreed, was the signing of the Declaration of Independence in 1776.

Other major events were the surrender of the British army at Yorktown in 1781, and the defeat of Burgoyne at Saratoga in 1777. Also important were scenes Trumbull had already painted: the Battle of Bunker Hill and the siege of Quebec in 1775, and Washington's victories at Trenton in 1776 and Princeton in 1777.

General Washington's willing resignation as commander-in-chief in 1783 was perhaps the most significant event of all. This single act symbolized the principle that America's elected civilian government was superior to its military leadership. Portraying this remarkable moment appealed strongly to Trumbull, who so loved and respected Washington for all he had done to establish their young republic.

The Soldiers' Artist

Jefferson helped with the concept for the Declaration picture, sketching the interior of Independence Hall in Philadelphia. He described the key moment when the committee, which he led with Benjamin Franklin and John Adams, presented the final draft of the Declaration to the Continental Congress. This act severed colonial ties with Great Britain. If the Patriots had been defeated, almost everyone in that chamber would have been executed or imprisoned for treason.

Jefferson now invited many of the French generals who had been at Yorktown to visit his home in Paris. There they readily posed for Trumbull, and he began to "collect heads" for his historical pictures. Jefferson also sat for his portrait, and he would do so more than once for Trumbull.

Over the next few years, Trumbull met most of the people in his Revolutionary scenes and painted their portraits, usually in miniature. Not only did he insist on accurately portraying his subjects, but he was determined to get the settings and even the soldiers' uniforms and gear correct. The authenticity of Trumbull's paintings and his dozens of portraits from life made him the most important artistic documentarian of the Revolutionary period.

The Finest Picture

In order to arrange for the best engravers of the day to copy his paintings, Trumbull departed for Germany at the end of summer 1786. He toured the Rhine country and passed through the Netherlands and Belgium, making his way back to England. When he arrived in London that November, he said, "my brain [was] half turned by the attention which had been paid to my paintings in Paris, and by the multitude of fine things I had seen."

In London, Trumbull was not as welcome, however. British society still resented the former Patriot officer, even though the war was over. His work met with little financial or critical success, even though during this time he painted what is often considered his finest historical picture. Ironically, this picture is of a British victory.

Trumbull showed British forces in action during the 1781 Spanish siege of the Fortress of Gibraltar. He painted the moment of triumph when the British broke out in a successful counterattack. *The Sortie Made by the Garrison of Gibraltar* went on exhibit in mid-1789.

Trumbull was pleased when the picture attracted public attention "in a satisfactory degree," despite his reputation as a former American rebel. "The military were partial to it," he wrote, "and I seldom looked into the room without being cheered by the sight of groups of officers of the Guards, in their splendid uniforms."

The attendance of officers at the exhibit came to an abrupt end, however, when a prominent lord who had served in the Revolution objected to Trumbull, saying, "[N]othing by that man ought to be patronized by officers of the British Army." On the other hand, Horace Walpole, the "celebrated connoisseur" and statesman, told West that this was "the finest picture he had ever seen, painted on the northern side of the Alps."

Following spread: In *The Sortie Made by the Garrison of Gibraltar,* the dying soldier (center) was a Spanish officer who had charged the British single-handedly after his men retreated.

The Sortie Made by the Garrison of Gibraltar. John Trumbull, 1789

The beginning of the French Revolution in 1789, when the political prisoners held at the Bastille were freed, is now celebrated as a French national holiday. Trumbull was in France at the time and saw many such violent scenes firsthand.

CHAPTER SIX

A World of Revolution and War

In such a state of things, what hope remained for the arts? None—my great enterprise was blighted.
—John Trumbull

Between 1787 and 1789, Trumbull visited Jefferson twice in Paris. They continued to develop ideas for historical paintings of the Revolution.

As Trumbull made plans to return to America in 1789 to "collect the heads" of famous Patriots, Jefferson offered him the position of secretary. Trumbull was grateful for the offer, which would have allowed him to live and work in France with few financial worries. He turned it down, however, because he was determined to return to America.

Trumbull hoped, as he put it, for "the warm patronage of my countrymen" to further his career. Also, he was worried about being caught up in France's worsening revolutionary conflict. Trumbull thought the French would soon force King Louis XVI to give up absolute power and establish a republic. He only hoped it would not involve violence and bloodshed. The American Revolution had lasted twenty years—from the mid-1760s until 1783—but the actual fighting had been limited and the deaths relatively few.

Earlier that year, Trumbull and Lafayette had helped calm an angry mob threatening to attack French aristocrats' homes. Trumbull was in Paris in the fall when another mob destroyed the hated Bastille prison, a symbol of royal oppression of the people.

No one knew what would happen in France if the people rebelled. There was no telling how many would suffer before such a struggle ended.

Most European countries opposed the French Revolution and later the reign of Napoleon Bonaparte, causing a widespread war in Europe that lasted until 1815. This 1850 historical painting illustrates the devastation of the battles.

By late November 1789, Trumbull had sailed across the Atlantic Ocean and was back in New York City. Jefferson also returned to America at this time, intending to go back to France, though he never would.

A Revolutionary against the Mob

Trumbull reported on his experiences in Paris to George Washington, now president of the newly established United States. Already, news had arrived of the spreading violence in France. Aristocrats were being murdered by rioters. The uprising threatened to destroy the French aristocracy—some of whom had been Trumbull's generous hosts. He was shocked that the French Revolution was turning so bloody and ruthless.

Trumbull soon gave up his plan for selling copies or engravings of his Revolutionary War paintings in France. The savagery of the revolution appalled him. "The beautiful theory [of the American Revolution] had been subverted—France had been overwhelmed in crime, and deluged with blood—the king had been beheaded, [and] Lafayette himself had been exiled." Trumbull's hopes for France were fading, but he expected his career to prosper in America. He was thirty-three years old.

While favoring a republican form of government, Trumbull did not agree with stirring up mob action to achieve it. Also, he believed in human liberty but would never wish to lose his own social standing as an American aristocrat. In addition, it was members of the wealthy and refined part of society who could afford to support artists.

Much of Europe burst into flames, as France fought Great Britain and several other nations. European monarchs were determined to prevent France from leading the way to republicanism, while French revolutionaries were eager to spread their struggle to every other monarchy in the world.

The people of the United States were sharply divided for or against the French Revolution. It troubled Trumbull that Jefferson, now the American secretary of state, was such a staunch supporter of the French Revolution with its immense bloodshed: "My whole soul revolted from the atrocities of France, while he approved or apologized for all. . . . [A] coldness gradually [came between us]." Trumbull declined Jefferson's offer to serve as ambassador to the Barbary States of the North African coast.

Lost Love, Abandoned Art

As he had planned, Trumbull journeyed up and down the eastern seaboard to sketch portraits of famous Patriots for his historical paintings. In 1790, he painted another full-length portrait of Washington, the person he admired most of all.

Trumbull was in love with Harriet Wadsworth, a childhood friend. When she did not accept his proposal of marriage, he cherished the hope that she would one day change her mind. Harriet was sickly, however, and died in 1793.

Harriet's death caused Trumbull deep sorrow. Combined with the horrors of the French Revolution, her death made him so miserable that he stopped work on his paintings. Also, it seemed that the revolution itself was sinking into the distant past. Americans showed little interest in the people and events that had founded their nation. Unable to sell much work, Trumbull became ever more depressed and eventually gave up painting altogether. "In such a state of things," he wrote, "what hope remained for the arts? None—my great enterprise was blighted."

In this unhappy period, Trumbull had a brief affair with Temperance Ray, a servant in his brother Jonathan's house. The result was the birth in 1792 of a son, whom he arranged to give to a family that could afford to raise him and give him a proper education. Money was provided to care for the boy, named John Trumbull Ray, by his mother.

Trumbull was among the first artists to paint Niagara Falls in western New York, portraying its spectacular torrent in several landscapes. He called them "panorama Views" of a "Scene magnificent & novel."

Resuming His Pencils

In 1794, Trumbull accepted an offer to join United States diplomat John Jay, who was to negotiate an important treaty between the United States and Britain. Jay led the American delegation to London.

Since France and Britain were at war, the French objected to the United States negotiating a separate treaty with Britain. During his service with the Jay commission, Trumbull traveled to France to communicate with American officials there. Many of the French aristocrats he had known in happier times were either banished or dead. Trumbull found himself no longer welcome in France, and returned to London.

Matters between France and the United States steadily worsened, and in 1796 a brief, undeclared naval war broke out. Each attacked the other's merchant vessels, at great expense to both sides, until they reached a peace agreement. Trumbull's service with the Jay commission drew to a close at this time, and he found himself anxious to take up painting once more—"to resume my Pencils," as he put it.

Sarah and John

On a happy day in 1800 in London, John Trumbull married Sarah Hope Harvey, a pretty Scottish-born woman who had been raised in England as an orphan. Sarah had no special standing in society, so she could not introduce her husband to possible clients. Yet Trumbull loved her and considered her his closest friend.

Gossip swirled about the new Mrs. Trumbull, who was said to have been secretly divorced. Some believed she and Trumbull had been having an affair, and that when

Niagara Falls from Under Table Rock. John Trumbull, 1808

Sarah Trumbull with a Spaniel. John Trumbull, c. 1802

Trumbull painted this portrait of his wife, Sarah Hope Harvey Trumbull, in 1802. It was common in portraits of married women to include a dog, which symbolized the couple's faithfulness to each other.

TRUMBULL'S EYESIGHT

Throughout his career, John Trumbull had the difficulty of being "monocular," able to see only with one eye. This meant that it was difficult to paint in large scale. In large pictures, the relationship between closer and more distant objects was hard for him to see and paint.

Trumbull worked best in smaller scale. The Battle of Bunker's Hill and Attack on Quebec, his first two historical pictures—perhaps his best—were both about three feet wide. He seldom painted life-sized subjects, so it is remarkable that his most enduring legacy is his oversized murals. Trumbull created these huge paintings between 1818 and 1824, despite the difficulties caused by his monocular vision.

Benjamin West knew of Trumbull's problem with perspective on large pictures. The elder artist advised him to paint only smaller canvases. In 1790, Trumbull wrote West to say he was about to "disobey one of your injunctions" and paint a life-sized portrait of General Washington for the city of New York. That seven-foot-tall picture, along with a number of other Trumbull portraits, hangs in City Hall.

In 1827, Trumbull told a friend, "[I will] devote myself without intermission" to continuing the Revolutionary series as "small paintings." He said, "With the aid of the Optician I can still execute such small work." Those pictures were in the collection bequeathed to the Trumbull Gallery at Yale.

her wealthy husband discovered it, he gave her a secret divorce to avoid scandal. These stories were never proven, but when the Trumbulls returned to America in 1804, rumors followed them. Although some family members accepted Sarah, others were cool to her.

For four years, the Trumbulls tried to make their way in America, first in Boston, then in New York. They traveled through the countryside, Trumbull sketching and painting, often landscapes. In these years, artists were turning away from religious and historical subjects and instead painting the natural world. America's untamed wilderness beckoned to many young landscape painters. Although he was no longer young, Trumbull was attracted by the spirit of the times. He ventured into nature for his subjects rather than into his memory of historical events.

Several of Trumbull's ambitious pictures were of Niagara Falls, among the first paintings of this great natural wonder. Sarah modeled for some of her husband's pictures, notably religious scenes taken from stories in the Bible. Trumbull painted her portrait at least a dozen times. They were happily married but would never have children of their own.

Meanwhile, John Trumbull Ray was being raised in western New York State. Sarah knew about John and accepted him as part of the family. She and Trumbull named him their nephew and the heir to lands Trumbull owned in New York State. John Ray was becoming a tall, handsome young man, who resembled his father. There would be no further communication with Ray's mother, whose life as a servant was distant from the privileged world of John Trumbull.

War Again with Great Britain

Unfortunately, Trumbull made little money from his latest work. The American economy was suffering from France's ongoing conflict with the rest of the world—known as the Napoleonic Wars after the French emperor, Napoleon Bonaparte. By 1808, Trumbull was unhappy with life in America, and there was lack of interest in his art. He returned to London with Sarah.

Another reason for going to London was to find medical treatment for an "alarming decay" of his sight. His good eye was giving him problems, sometimes with blurry vision. Trumbull's eyes often were dry and inflamed, "troublesome but . . . not dangerous," he wrote to a friend.

Ray soon followed his "aunt and uncle" to England, where his father arranged for him to live on a farm and learn British agricultural methods. Instead, Ray dismayed his family by joining the British army. He served as an officer, fighting in the Napoleonic Wars. Ray eventually became a merchant seaman, traveling around the world. Although they corresponded for some years, father and son would never see each other again.

The longstanding threat of conflict between Britain and America became reality in 1812. Even though his son was serving in the British army, Trumbull was looked upon with suspicion at the outbreak of the War of 1812. Again an enemy alien, he was not permitted to leave England and had to report regularly to the government.

Feelings on both sides of the Atlantic ran high, and some considered the hostilities a second American war of independence. For the most part, the war went badly for the Americans. In August 1814, a British invasion force captured Washington, D.C., and burned most of the public buildings, including the Capitol and the White House.

By 1815, Napoleon had been defeated, and peace came to Europe. America and Britain also made peace, which allowed the Trumbulls to leave England. They immediately hurried back to the United States.

Etching of John Trumbull. Asher Brown Durand, c. 1850

Trumbull was always a distinguished figure when he strode the streets of New York City, where he lived in later life. This etching is based on a painting by Samuel Lovett Waldo and Matther Harris Jouett.

CHAPTER SEVEN

An Artist and a Gentleman

Trumbull is your painter; never neglect Trumbull.
—William Makepeace Thackeray

Portrait painting, once Trumbull's main employment, was difficult to come by in America in the early nineteenth century. The national economy still suffered from years of war, so few patrons could afford to have their portraits painted.

Also, there was considerable competition these days. Gilbert Stuart was the leading American portraitist, and more young men were rising in the profession. These included Samuel F.B. Morse (another former student of West's), Rembrandt Peale, and Washington Allston. Nevertheless, the aging Trumbull was a highly respected elder statesman among American painters.

More than sixty years old at a time when even fifty was considered elderly, Trumbull was one of the few surviving Revolutionary War officers. He retained vivid memories of that period and had collected all those portraits of the participants. He longed to paint the historical series for the government in Washington before he was too old.

Trumbull wrote to former presidents Jefferson and Adams, asking for their support: "Future artists may arise with far Superior Talents, but Time has already withdrawn almost all of their Models . . . no time remains therefore for hesitation."

Jefferson, in particular, backed Trumbull's cause. He told Congress that in Europe, Trumbull "was considered as superior to West [and] I thought him superior to any historical painter of the day except David."

Adams said he did not care for art, nor did he wish to remember the events of the Revolutionary War. President James Madison, however, agreed with Jefferson. Now

The United States Capitol was rebuilt early in the nineteenth century, when four of John Trumbull's great historical paintings of the American Revolution were hung in the Rotunda under the dome.

that the nation had come through a bitter war with Britain, thoughts of the Revolutionary triumph stirred. A newborn patriotism inspired Americans, who wanted to honor the events of the nation's founding years.

While Trumbull awaited the decision of the national government, New York artists and patrons established the American Academy of Fine Arts in 1816. Trumbull was the most prominent artist in the American Academy's first exhibit. He became an Academy director and then vice president. At last, in January 1817, Congress commissioned Trumbull to paint four paintings for the Capitol Rotunda. Situated beneath a proposed dome, the Rotunda was designed to be the physical heart of the Capitol.

A Patriotic Duty

Trumbull set out to portray the presentation of the Declaration of Independence, Burgoyne's surrender at Saratoga, Cornwallis's surrender at Yorktown, and the resignation of General Washington. These were the subjects that he and Jefferson had discussed in Paris in 1786.

The task was a difficult one, for the Rotunda pictures would be extremely large—12 feet tall and 18 feet wide (3.7 meters by 5.5 meters). They would be like murals, or wall paintings. The figures were to be "as large as life," according to the agreement with Congress. For his work, Trumbull would be paid the impressive sum of $32,000, or $8,000 per picture, in four installments. It was more than he had ever before received for a painting.

This commission would be extremely challenging. His advanced age would make the physical labor on such large pictures exhausting. His previous historical pictures had been relatively small, about three feet wide.

Also, having only one good eye would make it difficult to paint so wide an image with the proper perspective and proportions. Depth of field—the relationship between objects in the front and back of the scene—would be hard for him to judge.

As Trumbull bravely pushed on with his task at his studio in New York, the design and construction of the Capitol Rotunda was under way. The leading architect, Charles Bulfinch, was a friend of Trumbull's from their days in Paris. Trumbull was soon shocked to hear that the original plan for a dome and a great circular room—a rotunda—was to be scrapped.

Saying he felt "the deepest regret" to hear this news, Trumbull explained to Bulfinch how a rotunda and dome would offer the best light for the pictures. As he sketched his own ideas for design and construction, his love of architectural design came through strongly. Eventually, Bulfinch reworked his own design, earning Trumbull's gratitude for saving the "grand room."

Artist and architect discussed the Rotunda and placement of the pictures. Trumbull requested that the picture frames be decorated with "simple architectural foliage" and sketched a pattern for the leaves. He objected to using "Eagles and all those" bulky "ornaments which call the Eye from its proper object and . . . cast heavy and false Shadows on the Painting."

Bulfinch and Trumbull were in agreement for the most part as they discussed the placement of staircases and the relationship of windows to pictures. On one important point, however, Trumbull could not win. He was concerned that the Rotunda's design allowed too much humid night air into the gallery. This, he insisted, would promote

The Declaration of Independence, July 4, 1776. John Trumbull, 1819

Trumbull traveled around America to capture the likenesses of the Continental Congress delegates who had signed the Declaration of Independence in Philadelphia in July 1776.

Not only did Trumbull strive for accurate portraits in this scene of General Horatio Gates accepting General Burgoyne's surrender in 1777, but the artist also closely studied uniforms and equipment.

The Surrender of General Burgoyne at Saratoga, October 16, 1777. John Trumbull, c. 1822

The Surrender of Lord Cornwallis at Yorktown, October 19, 1781.
John Trumbull, 1820

During his years in Europe, Trumbull met many British and French officers who had been at Cornwallis's surrender at Yorktown. He always took the opportunity to ask that they sit for a portrait, keeping a copy that he used for this future work.

As he did to prepare for all his great paintings, Trumbull traveled to the scene of the event to sketch the local setting. He visited the State House in Annapolis, Maryland, before composing his painting of Washington's resignation.

Washington Resigning His Commission, Annapolis, December 23, 1783.
John Trumbull, c. 1824

mold and mildew growing on the pictures, sure to destroy them in just a few years.

The airflow pattern was, however, little changed by Trumbull's protests. In 1828, he would have to return to Washington to care for the pictures, which were suffering from humidity. They would be taken down, removed from their frames, and cleaned. Then the backs of the canvases would be sealed with a mixture of melted beeswax and oil of turpentine. So the capable John Trumbull not only helped design the Capitol, but he even saved his own great paintings from ruin.

A Demanding Mentor

For almost seven grueling years, until 1824, Trumbull carried out what he considered his "patriotic duty." One by one, he completed the Revolutionary War scenes. The first, in 1819, was *The Declaration of Independence*, which toured the country as a traveling exhibit and received much acclaim.

During his work on the Capitol pictures, Trumbull was elected president of the American Academy of Fine Arts. Although he was honest and kindly at heart, Trumbull was a strict mentor to younger artists. For example, he was not flexible when it came to allowing artists to use the Academy's studios freely or even to borrow its art works for copying. He was considered a dictatorial president and acquired the reputation of being a crotchety old man.

Trumbull was accused of failing to encourage younger artists—which, in many cases, was true. Yet he did support those he admired and considered truly talented. Artists such as Washington Allston, Daniel Huntington, Asher Durand, and Thomas Cole all received crucial help from Trumbull to advance their careers.

Within a few years, a number of artists would withdraw from the American Academy of Fine Arts and establish the National Academy of Design.

The Hand and Spirit of a Painter

In spring 1824, just as Trumbull was completing the final Capitol painting—*Washington Resigning his Commission*—Sarah died after an illness. She was fifty years old.

Losing his "faithful and beloved companion of . . . twenty-four years" was a severe blow to the artist. Trumbull's joy at finishing his great national work was not to be shared with his dear Sarah.

In 1826, the Capitol Rotunda opened to the public, with Trumbull's paintings the most prominent attractions. Thousands of visitors viewed these four famous events of the Revolution as portrayed by a man who had lived through those tumultuous times.

Sarah Trumbull (Sarah Hope Harvey) on Her Deathbed. John Trumbull, 1824

Trumbull was brokenhearted in 1824 at the death of his beloved Sarah, his "dearest friend." His strong religious convictions are revealed in this painting of Sarah on her deathbed, hands extended as if in appeal to a divine vision.

Although he was past his prime as an artist, and the large scale had given him difficulty, Trumbull's paintings were greatly admired.

One historian, who overheard younger artists Morse and Rembrandt Peale in a discussion about these paintings, recorded their opinions. Both regarded "Trumbull's four pictures as works of great intrinsic value, because of the portraits."

Some years later, the highly respected English author William Makepeace Thackeray came to the Rotunda. Himself an accomplished artist, Thackeray showed a close interest in the paintings. "He took a quiet turn around the rotunda," an American author wrote, "and in a few words gave each picture its perfectly correct rank and art valuation. 'Trumbull is your painter;' he said, 'never neglect Trumbull.'"

When Trumbull's paintings were mounted in 1826, four other Rotunda panels remained empty, panels he proposed to fill. He suggested calling the exhibition space the "Hall of the Revolution," and he was keenly disappointed when Congress turned down his proposal. The works of other artists would one day fill those panels.

Designing a Gallery and Graves

Again in ill health in 1830, Trumbull wondered what to do with the dozens of paintings he owned. He referred to them as "my children." As he said in his memoir, "[these] subjects of national history . . . have been the great objects of my professional life." Trumbull offered to sell his paintings and his own considerable collection of the works by the Old Masters to Yale College in New Haven, Connecticut.

Influential friends in the arts and at Yale raised the funds to build a new gallery dedicated to Trumbull. They agreed to pay him $1,000 a year for the rest of his life. The gallery also would receive newly painted versions of his Revolutionary War scenes.

The artist called on his own architectural talents and designed the gallery, which would also house his and Sarah's graves. The Trumbulls would be buried in a crypt under the building at the foot of one of his full-length portraits of George Washington, the man he called his "master."

When Yale's Trumbull Gallery opened in 1832, it was a widely hailed triumph, and thousands flocked to see it. The *Connecticut Journal* wrote: "Col. Trumbull has the hand and spirit of a painter. . . . Altogether this Gallery must be considered the most interesting collection of pictures in the country. They are American."

Worthy of Imitation

In 1836, Trumbull resigned as president of the American Academy of Fine Arts, which closed in 1841. This marked the end of the era of which he was a leading national symbol.

For the next few years, he worked on his memoir, *The Autobiography, Reminiscences and Letters of John Trumbull.* The book was published in 1841, with twenty-three illustrations. It was the first book-length autobiographical work published by an American artist.

John Trumbull died at his home in New York City on November 10, 1843, at the age of eighty-seven. He was buried alongside Sarah Hope Trumbull in the Trumbull Gallery at Yale. Among the obituaries was one by Thomas S. Cummings, a National Academy of Design member with whom Trumbull once had strong differences:

THE TRUMBULL GALLERY

John Trumbull sold twenty-eight paintings and sixty miniature portraits to Yale in December 1831. The gallery was built on what became Yale's "Old Campus." It opened in October 1832.

The patriot-artist was an accomplished amateur architect and had designed, among other structures, a meeting house in Lebanon, Connecticut, which still stands. For the gallery at Yale, he collaborated with professional architect and friend Ithiel Town, of New Haven.

The Trumbull Gallery has been described as "thoroughly functional . . . and in the mode of the moment." Connecticut sandstone composed the lower parts of the walls, and the upper portions were of cement.

The gallery's top floor had two main rooms, about 30 feet (9.1 meters) square and 15 feet (4.6 meters) high to the skylight. The north gallery held Trumbull's works, while the south gallery held paintings by other artists, including John Smibert and Samuel Morse.

In keeping with Trumbull's elegant style, the galleries were lined with pine planks for hanging the paintings. The pine was covered with red moreen, a sturdy cloth, mostly embossed with a design. The carpet was green, and there were settees, chairs, and stools made of maple, with cane seats.

As a fire-safety measure, the gallery floors had slits along the walls, so pictures could be dropped down and removed quickly. The slits were 12 feet (3.7 meters) long and 15 inches wide (38 centimeters) and concealed by a movable board covered by carpet.

The Trumbull Gallery was the first college art gallery in America. More than that, it was one of the earliest picture galleries in North America.

Departed this life, the venerable Colonel Trumbull, aged eighty-seven years— an artist and a gentleman. . . . He was of the old school; his courtesy and urbanity of manner were worthy of imitation.

A eulogy was given by Samuel Morse, another artist who had objected to Trumbull's strict control of the American Academy of Fine Arts. Morse said:

[Trumbull's] fame is interwoven, not merely with the history of the arts of design, but also with the political history of the country. . . . On numerous paint-

Trumbull's most famous paintings were reproduced as hand-colored engravings, such as this one of *The Declaration of Independence* issued by Currier and Ives. Reproductions of Trumbull's work were found in most homes in nineteenth-century America, and they still are, whether as color prints or in books about the history of the United States.

ings connected with our Revolutionary history, Colonel Trumbull's fame as an artist may securely rest.

Over time, Americans increasingly appreciated the enduring treasures that Trumbull had left them. He was honored as never before. As printing technology improved, his historical paintings would be reproduced in the thousands as Currier and Ives prints. Trumbull pictures would be framed to hang in most American homes, and for generations to come his artwork would regularly be reproduced in books and periodicals.

John Trumbull summed up his life with the inscription on his memorial in the Yale Gallery: "To his country he gave his sword and pencil."

GLOSSARY

Canvas—Closely woven cloth, usually of linen (cloth made of flax), stretched on a frame and used for paintings, especially those made with oil paints.

Capitol Rotunda—The central round building below the dome of the United States Capitol. Designed in 1793, it was begun in 1818 and completed in 1824.

Charcoal and wash study—A preliminary sketch for an oil painting in which lines are drawn with charcoal and a layer of diluted color—a wash—is brushed on.

Engraving—A picture created by cutting, or engraving, lines onto special wooden blocks, stone tablets, or metal plates, which are used to print the image on paper.

Glaze—A thin, transparent, or partly transparent coating painted over a picture to bring out certain colors or achieve particular effects, such as subduing a color's brightness or enhancing other elements.

Historical painting—A work that depicts an event in the past, usually an important event in progress or famous people in action.

Landscape painting—A picture that shows a view of a natural scene and is often dramatic or inspiring.

Limner—The term for a painter in the eighteenth century. Such an artist's work was known as limning, or illuminating.

Loyalist—An American who remained loyal to the British king and opposed the American Revolution.

Miniaturist—An artist who paints small pictures, usually portraits, on such surfaces as ivory for a locket or thin wood to be enclosed in an oval frame.

Palette—A thin board or tablet with a thumb hole, used for holding an artist's paints and for mixing pigments with oil.

Patriot—An American who fought against British colonial rule in the American Revolution.

Pencil—A seventeenth-century term for the artist's brushes. It also may refer to the profession of art, as in "to take up the pencil."

TIME LINE

1756: John Trumbull is born on June 6 in Lebanon, Connecticut.

1772–1773: Trumbull studies law at Harvard College.

1773: In December, troubles between America and Britain are brought to a head by the Boston Tea Party.

1775: The battles of Lexington and Concord in Massachusetts turn out the New England militia, including Trumbull's company, to besiege the British in Boston.

1775–1776: After serving as an aide to Washington during the siege of Boston, Trumbull is appointed colonel.

1777: Trumbull resigns from the militia.

1778: He studies in Boston with students of John Singleton Copley.

1780: Trumbull sails to Paris, then to London to study with Benjamin West. In November, he is arrested as a Patriot who fought against the British and imprisoned for eight months; upon his release, he returns home.

1784: Trumbull goes back to London to resume study with West and begins to develop historical pictures.

1792: Trumbull's son, John Trumbull Ray, is born out of wedlock to Temperance Ray.

1795–1798: Trumbull travels in Europe to help negotiate a shipping treaty between America and France; he then returns to England.

1800: Trumbull marries Scottish-born Englishwoman Sarah Hope Harvey.

1804: Trumbull and Sarah go to America.

1808: Trumbull returns with Sarah to England.

1812–1815: The United States is at war with Great Britain, whose forces burn the Capitol at Washington, D.C. In 1815, Trumbulls return to America.

1817: Trumbull is elected president of the American Academy of Fine Arts and is commissioned to paint four historical works for the Rotunda of the Capitol.

1824: His wife, Sarah, dies at the age of fifty.

1826: The Capitol Rotunda featuring Trumbull's four historical paintings is open to the public.

1832: The Trumbull Gallery opens at Yale College in New Haven, Connecticut, with twenty-eight of his paintings and sixty miniature portraits.

1837: Trumbull begins to write his autobiography. It will be published in 1841.

1843: Trumbull dies on November 10, at his home in New York City.

FURTHER RESEARCH

ABOUT HIS LIFE

John Trumbull: Artist of the Revolution
www.earlyamerica.com/review/summer/trumbull.html

ABOUT HIS PAINTING

Declaration of Independence by John Trumbull
www.ushistory.org/declaration/trumbull.htm

Interactive John Trumbull's Declaration of Independence
www.quiz-tree.com/Declaration-of-Independence-Trumbull.html

Paintings in the Rotunda
www.aoc.gov/cc/photo-gallery/ptgs_rotunda.cfm

Wright, Tricia. *American Art and Artists.* New York: HarperCollins, 2007; Washington, DC: Smithsonian Institution, 2007.

ABOUT THE PERIOD

Bliven, Bruce, Jr. *The American Revolution.* New York: Random House, 1981.

Miller, Brandon Marie. *Life During the American Revolution.* Minneapolis, MN: Lerner, 2005.

Murray, Stuart. *American Revolution.* New York: DK Publishing, 2005.

BIBLIOGRAPHY

BOOKS

Cooper, Helen A. et al. *John Trumbull: The Hand and Spirit of a Painter*. New Haven, CT: Yale University Art Gallery, 1982.

Jaffe, Irma B. *John Trumbull: Patriot-Artist of the American Revolution*. Boston: New York Graphic Society, 1975.

Sizer, Theodore, ed. *The Works of Colonel John Trumbull*. New Haven, CT: Yale University Press, 1967.

Trumbull, John. *The Autobiography of Colonel John Trumbull, Patriot-Artist, 1756–1843*. 1841. Ed. Theodore Sizer. New Haven, CT: Yale University Press, 1953.

ARTICLES

Dillon, Keira. "The Complicated Relationship Between John Trumbull and Native Americans." Fordham University Libraries. www.library.fordham.edu/trumbull/conflict.html

Favata, Daniel C. "John Trumbull: A Founding Father of American Art." Fordham University Libraries. www.library.fordham.edu/trumbull/founding.html

Heleniak, Kathryn Moore. "Benjamin West and John Trumbull." Fordham University Libraries. www.library.fordham.edu/trumbull/benjamin.html

Jaffe, Irma B. "Preface to John Trumbull: A Founding Father of American Art." Fordham University Libraries. www.library.fordham.edu/trumbull/preface.html

WEB SITES

Guide to pictures of works by John Trumbull in art museum sites and image archives worldwide
www.artcyclopedia.com/artists/trumbull_john.html

John Trumbull: Artist of the Revolution
www.earlyamerica.com/review/summer/trumbull.html

National Gallery of Art
www.nga.gov/cgi-bin/pbio?30800

Trumbull Gallery at Yale
www.yalealumnimagazine.com/issues/01_03/popup/landmarks/7.html

SOURCE NOTE

Most of the quotations in this book come from Trumbull's 1841 autobiography. The author consulted the 1953 edition, which has a preface by Theodore Sizer.

INDEX

Page numbers in *italics* refer to illustrations.

Adams, Abigail, 41, 44

Adams, John, *10*, 11, 50, 63

Allston, Washington, 38, 63, 68

American Academy of Fine Arts, 12, 64, 70

American Revolution, paintings of battles, *2–3*, *17*, *18*, *20*, *21*, *22*, *28*, *31*, *40*, *42–43*, *46–47*, *49*, *52–53*, *64*, *65*

American School, The (Pratt), *34*

Analysis of Beauty (Hogarth), 32

André, John, 36

Architecture, 12–13, 71

Arnold, Benedict, 22, 36, *47*

Arrests, 37

Autobiography, Reminiscences and Letters of John Trumbull, The (Trumbull), 70

Bastille prison, *54*, 55

Battle of Lexington, The (Wollen), *17*

Benjamin Franklin (Trumbull), *33*

Bonaparte, Napoleon, 56, 61

Boston, Massachusetts, 16–21, 29–30, 32–33

Boston Tea Party, 16

Bulfinch, Charles, 65

Bunker Hill, Battle of, 19–20, *20*, 21–22, *42–43*, 44–45, 49

Burgoyne, John, 27, 29, *31*, 50, 66

Burke, Edmund, 37

Canada, invasion of, 21–22, *22*, 44, 49, 50

Cannae, Battle of, 16

Capitol Rotunda. *See* Rotunda pictures

Capture of the Hessians at Trenton, The (Trumbull), *40*

Champlain, Lake, 22, 25

Clothing, 15, 20

Cole, Thomas, 68

Colonel rank, 22–23, 25

Colors, use of, 32

Combat at Quiberon Bay in 1795 (Sorieul), *56*

Concord, Battle of, 17

Continental Congress, *10*, 66

Copley, John Singleton, 15, 16, *16*, 29, 36, 38, 41

Cornwallis, Charles, *18*, 39, *67*

Cosway, Maria, 45, 48

Cosway, Richard, 45, *48*

Cummings, Thomas S., 70–71

Currier and Ives prints, 72, *72*

David, Jacques Louis, 45, 49, 63

Death of General Mercer at the Battle of Princeton, January 3, 1777, The (Trumbull), *21*, 49

Death of General Montgomery in Attack on Quebec, December 31, 1775, The (Trumbull), *22*, 47

Death of General Warren at the Battle of Bunker's Hill, June 17, 1775, The (Trumbull), *2–3*, *20*, *42–43*

Death of General Wolfe, The (West), *29*

Death of John Trumbull, 70

Declaration of Independence, *10*, 50, 65, 66, 68, 72

Declaration of Independence, July 4, 1776, The (Trumbull), *10*, *66*, 68, *72*

Defiance, Mount, 22, 27

Dogs, as symbols in portraits, 59

Dunlap, William, 38

Durand, Asher Brown, *62*, 68

Earl, Ralph, 38

Elliott, Charlie Loring, 11–13

Emerson, Ralph Waldo, 17

Etching of John Trumbull (Durand), *62*

Executions, 36, 37

Eyesight, 61, 65

Fashion, 15, 20

First Connecticut Regiment, 19–20

Fox, Charles J., 37

Franklin, Benjamin, *10*, 32, 33, *33*, 50

French Revolution, *54*, 55–57, *56*

Gates, Horatio, 22

General George Washington at Trenton (Trumbull), *24*

George III (King of England), 13, 29, 36, 37

Germany, 51

Gibraltar, siege of fortress of, 51, *52–53*

Gilbert Stuart (West), *38*

Gore, Christopher, 29
Graves of Trumbull and wife, 70

Hall of the Revolution, 70
Hancock, John, *10*, 25
Harvard College, 14–15
Harvey, Sarah Hope (wife). *See* Trumbull, Sarah
Hogarth, William, 32
Houdon, Jean Antoine, 45, 49
Hudson River, 27
Humidity damaging paintings, 68
Huntington, Daniel, 68

Jay, John, 58
Jefferson, Thomas, *10*, 11, 45, *48*, 50, 55, 57, 63
John Singleton Copley (Copley), *16*
Jonathan Trumbull, Jr. with Mrs. Trumbull (Eunice Backus) and Faith Trumbull (Trumbull), *14*
Jouett, Matther Harrie, 62

King, Rufus, 29
Kings, *see names of Kings*

Lafayette, Marquis de, 11, 45, 55, 56–57
Languages, talent for, 13–14, 16
Lexington, Battle of, 17, *17*
Livingston, Robert R., *10*
London, England
    John Singleton Copley, 16, 29
    move to, 32–33
    painting in, 35–37
    returning to, 39, 41, 51, 61
Louis XVI (King of France), 55

Madison, James, 63
Madonna della Sedia (Raphael), 36
Map of American Revolutionary battles painted by Trumbull, *8–9*
Mercer, Hugh, *21*, 49
Miniature portraits, 45, *48*, 50, 71
Monroe, James, 11
Montgomery, Richard, *22*, 47
Morse, Samuel F.B., 7, 38, 63, 69, 71–72

Napoleonic Wars, 61
Native Americans, 27
Nature paintings, 60
New York City, 22, 39, 56

Niagara Falls, *58–59*, 60
Niagara Falls from Under Table Rock (Trumbull), *58–59*

Paris, France, 33, 45, 49–50, 55
Patriot soldiers, *see* American Revolution, paintings of battles; Washington, George; *other American commanders*
Peale, Charles Willson, 32, 38
Peale, Rembrandt, 63, 69
Poussin, Nicholas, 30
Portraits of Trumbull, 6, *26*, *62*
Pratt, Matthew, *34*, 38
Princeton, Battle of, *21*, *49*, 50
Prison, 37

Quebec siege, 21–22, *22*, 44, 49, 50

Raphael, 30, 36
Ray, John Trumbull (son), 57, 60–61
Ray, Temperence, 57, 61
Redcoats, *see* American Revolution, paintings of battles; *British commanders*
Religious paintings, 60
Rembrandt, 50
Resignation of General Washington's Commission, Annapolis, December 23, 1783, The (Trumbull), *67*
Revolutionary War, *see* American Revolution, paintings of battles
Reynolds, Joshua, 41, 44
Rhode Island, 25, 30
Rome, 38
Rotunda pictures
    Burgoyne's surrender at Saratoga, *31*, 50, 65, 66
    Cornwallis's surrender at Yorktown, *18*, 50, 65, 67
    overview of, 64–70, *64*
    resignation of George Washington, 50, 65, 67, 68
    signing of Declaration of Independence, *10*, 66, 68, *72*
Royal Academy of Arts, 38, 41, 50
Rubens, Peter Paul, 50

Sarah Trumbull (Sarah Jope Harvey) on Her Deathbed (Trumbull), 69
Sarah Trumbull with a Spaniel (Trumbull), 59
Saratoga, defeat of Burgoyne at, 27, 29, *31*, 50, 65, 66

Self-Portrait (Trumbull), *26*
Seniority in Revolutionary army, 25
Sherman, Roger, *10*
Sight, 61, 65
Sizer, Theodore, 7
Smibert, John, 30, 71
Sorieul, Jean, *56*
Sortie Made by the Garrison of Gibraltar, The
    (Trumbull), 51, *52–53*
Spirit of '76 (Willard), *28*
Spying, 20, 33
Storming of the Bastille, July 14, 1789 (Thevenin),
    54
Stuart, Gilbert, 36, 38, *38*, 63
Sullivan, John, 30
Sully, Thomas, 38
*Surrender of General Burgoyne at Saratoga, October
    16, 1777, The* (Trumbull), *31*, 66
*Surrender of Lord Cornwallis at Yorktown, October
    19, 1781, The* (Trumbull), *18*, 67

Thackeray, William Makepeace, 63, 69
Thevenin, Charles, *54*
Thomas Jefferson (Trumbull), *48*
Ticonderoga, Fort, 22–25, 27
Tisdale, Nathan, 13, 16
Tothill Fields Bridewell, 37
Town, Ithiel, 71
Treason, 35, 36, 37
Trenton, Battle of, *24*, *40*, 50
Trumbull, Eunice Backus (sister-in-law), *14*
Trumbull, Faith (niece), *14*
Trumbull, Faith (sister), 19
Trumbull, Jonathan (father), 13, 15, 16, 39, 44, 45
Trumbull, Jonathan, Jr. (brother), *14*, 15, 44, 57
Trumbull, Sarah (wife), 58–61, *59*, 68–69, *69*, 70

Trumbull Gallery, 70, 71
Tyler, Royal, 30

Van Dyck, Anthony, 30
Vaudreuil, Comte de, 45
Vesuvius, Mount, 15
Vision, 61, 65

Wadsworth, Harriet, 57
Waldo, Samuel Lovett, 62
Walpole, Horace, 37, 51
War of 1812, 61
Warren, Joseph, *20*, *42–43*, 44–45
Washington, D.C., burning of, 61
Washington, George, 56
    paintings of, 11, *21*, *24*, *32*, *40*, *67*, *70*
    resignation of as commander-in-chief, 50, 65, *67*,
       68
    working for, 19, 20–21, 23, 39, 40
Washington Resigning His Commission (Trumbull),
    67, 68
West, Benjamin
    Gilbert Stuart (West), *38*
    imprisonment of Trumbull, 37
    praise from, 35, 44
    studios of, *34*, 38
    studying with, 33, 35–36, 39, 41
    success of in Britain, 29
    use of color by, 32
Willard, Archibald M., *28*
Windsor Castle, 41
Wollen, William Barnes, *17*

Yale College, 70, 71
"Year of the Bloody Sevens," 27
Yorktown, surrender of British army at, *18*, 50, 65, *67*

ABOUT THE AUTHOR

Stuart A.P. Murray has written many books, both fiction and nonfiction, for young readers. Among his books on the American Revolutionary period are *The Revolutionary War, America's Song: The Story of "Yankee Doodle," Washington's Farewell,* and *The Honor of Command: General Burgoyne's Saratoga Campaign.* John Trumbull's paintings have illustrated Murray's books and brought a sense of immediacy to the story that only Trumbull—the Revolution's ideal eyewitness and artist—could bring. Murray lives in Petersburgh, New York.

PHOTO CREDITS